THE **TESTING** SERIES

MAGISTRATE
INTERVIEW
QUESTIONS
AND ANSWERS

THE **TESTING** SERIES
expert advice on test preparation

Orders: Please contact How2become Ltd, Suite 2, 50 Churchill Square Business Centre, Kings Hill, Kent ME19 4YU.

You can also order via the e mail address info@how2become.co.uk.

ISBN: 9781907558337

First published 2012

Typeset for How2become Ltd by Molly Hill, Canada.

Printed in Great Britain for How2become Ltd by Bell & Bain Ltd, 303 Burnfield Road, Thornliebank, Glasgow G46 7UQ.

INTRODUCTION AND WELCOME

Welcome to your new guide, **The Magistrate Interview Questions and Answers**. This guide has been designed to help you prepare for and pass the magistrate interviews in England and Wales. The questions and answers contained within this guide are relevant for both the first and second interview. Once you have passed the first interview for becoming a magistrate you will be required to attend a second interview. The interviews are different in nature and both will require differing sets of skills which I will cover during the guide.

The selection process to become a magistrate is highly competitive. Armed with this insider's guide you have certainly taken the first step to passing the interviews for this important and highly responsible role.

The guide contains a number of sample interview questions and answers which are designed to help you to prepare. Read the questions and answers carefully and take notes as you progress. It is important to point out at the early stage that you **should not copy the examples** provided in the answers to the questions, but alternatively use them as a basis for your own preparation. It is essential that you provide responses to the questions that are based on your *own* individual experiences and opinions.

Don't ever give up on your dreams; if you really want to become a magistrate then you can do it. The way to approach the first interview is to embark on a programme of 'in-depth' preparation, and this guide will show you exactly how to do that.

I strongly advise that you develop your own skills and experiences around the six key qualities that are required for the role. You should also aim to provide as much 'evidence' as possible when responding to the interview questions. Many candidates who apply to become a magistrate will be unaware that the six key qualities even exist. As you progress through this guide you will find that these important elements of the role will form the foundations of your preparation.

So, the first step in your preparation, and before we go any further, is to get hold of a copy of the six key qualities that are required to become a magistrate. They will usually form part of your application pack but if they don't, you can obtain a copy of them by visiting the relevant Government website.

If you need any further help with any elements of the selection process, including application form and interview, then we offer a wide range of products to assist you. These are all available through our online shop www.how2become.co.uk.

We also run a series on 1-Day magistrate training courses. Details of which can be found here:

WWW.MAGISTRATECOURSE.CO.UK

Once again, thank you for your custom and we wish you every success in your pursuit to becoming a magistrate.

Work hard, stay focused and be what you want…

Best wishes,

The how2become team

The How2become Team

THE SIX KEY QUALITIES

Before we get in to the main element of the guide I want to cover the most important aspect of the first interview – being able to demonstrate the key qualities required to become a magistrate.

If you fail to provide evidence of where you meet the qualities you will not progress to the second interview, it's as simple as that.

Local Advisory Committees are the group of people who are responsible for the Appointment of Magistrates. Part of their role is to assess you against the 'Six Key Qualities'.

These are set out in the notes accompanying application forms that will form part of your application pack and are as follows:

1. **Good character**

   - Personal integrity
   - Respect and trust of others
   - Respect for confidences
   - Absence of any matter which might bring them or the magistracy into disrepute
   - Willingness to be circumspect in private, working and public life.

2. **Understanding and communication**

   - Ability to understand documents
   - Identify and comprehend relevant facts

- Follow evidence and arguments
- Ability to concentrate
- Ability to communicate effectively

3. **Social awareness**

   - Appreciation and acceptance of the Rule of Law (this is the fundamental principle that no one is above the law and that everyone is subject to it in equal measure)
   - Understanding of society in general
   - Respect for people from different ethnic, cultural or social backgrounds (and maybe some knowledge of 'other communities')
   - Awareness and understanding of life beyond family, friends and work is highly desirable
   - As is an understanding of your local community.

4. **Maturity and sound temperament**

   - Ability to relate to and work with others
   - Regard for the views of others
   - Willingness to consider advice
   - Humanity, firmness, decisiveness, confidence, a sense of fairness, courtesy.

5. **Sound judgement**

   - Ability to think logically, weigh arguments and reach a balanced decision
   - Openness of mind, objectivity, the recognition of and controlling of prejudices.

6. **Commitment and reliability**

   - Reliability, commitment to serve the community, willingness to undertake at least 26 half day sittings a year (but possibly more in practice)
   - Willingness to undertake the required training
   - Ability to offer the requisite time
   - Support of family and employer
   - Sufficiently good health.

For most practical purposes these will be the only matters that Advisory Committees are required and permitted to assess during the first interview. However, there are a large number of questions that could be asked centred on the six qualities. I will provide you as many as possible during a later chapter of this workbook.

In the next section of the workbook we will consider how and when the Advisory Committees assess these qualities and how you might best prepare yourself to give a demonstrably considered reply at interview.

You need to be aware from the offset that, during the application form and at both sets of interviews, you will also be asked what used to be called the 'Key Question' but is now known as the 'Good Character and Background Question' which is outlined below. Only you will know how to respond to this question but my advice is that your response needs to be an honest one.

Is there anything in your private or working life or in your past, or to your knowledge in that of any member of your family or close friends, which, if it became generally known, might bring you or the magistracy into disrepute, or call into question your integrity, authority or standing as a magistrate?

SOME THINGS TO DO

- Make sure that you are familiar with all aspects of the six key qualities and how you might demonstrate them at interview as part of your general approach to things that you may be asked about;

- Consider how you will answer the 'Good Character and Background Question' (you might end up answering it on three separate occasions);

- Consider the three competences and whether you are ready, after appointment and following training etc, for the process of being appraised on these.

Let us now move on to the first interview and how you can prepare for it.

THE FIRST INTERVIEW

Although being called for a first interview is a positive and encouraging event it must be remembered that:

- applicants whose paperwork is in order and who are not automatically disqualified will often receive a first interview as a matter of course

- this first interview will last for only around 35-40 minutes, so you will have to be highly focused on what is likely to be covered.

The interview will be held in a public building (often, but not necessarily, a courthouse) and the panel will comprise three (or, exceptionally, two) members, one of whom will usually be a non-magistrate, so the latter may come at matters very differently from the magistrate members. He or she will be an ordinary member of the public just as you are and may ask more general questions of the kind that concern ordinary people, especially in and around the town, city or rural area where you live or work. You can only really prepare for this by being alive to the key issues and debates that are current in your own community and society in general.

But try to think 'objective opinion' rather than 'overtly political stance'. Justice itself is 'politics' neutral and if you join the bench you will be surprised at how people with sometimes strong and differing political opinions come together to look at matters jointly, in a fair and even-handed way, free of preconceptions. Try to show that you can do this.

If you do need to offer a personal view because not to do so might make you seem a bit indifferent, try adding, in your own words, something to the effect of 'But that's my view and I realise that on the bench I will need to keep it to myself and look at things even-handedly and in a more rounded way'. This kind of reaction ought to be second nature; just as you should be careful never to denigrate or single out people who are 'different'. Everyone must be treated with human dignity and all points of view respected.

Interviews are usually not overly formal and the panel may introduce themselves by their forenames and may even ask if you are happy with that form of address – the aim is to be respectful and dignified but not stuffy.

You do not need 'to buy a new outfit' for the occasions, but do dress and conduct yourself in such a way as to show respect for the process and the role you are seeking to undertake. Because courts are solemn places dealing with things that affect other people's lives, a convention of 'sober dress' is generally observed, but equally this is a modern day and age. The last thing you want to do is look as if you have been kitted out by the 'props department'. You will have already seen magistrates in court during your observation visit(s) and this should have removed any misleading stereotypes that you may have had I mind.

The first interview will concentrate on four main aspects:

- checking, updating and exploring further what was on the original application form

- putting the 'Good Character and Background' question fairly early on

- concentrating on matters such as criminal justice issues and your pre-interview court visits/observations

- the two 'demonstrated/not demonstrated' Key Qualities of 'Commitment and Reliability' and 'Good Character'.

However, preliminary views will be formed on all six of the Key Qualities insofar as the opportunity to assess them has arisen - so do keep all six in mind.

Advisory Committees try to give each applicant a broadly similar interview experience. Locally, they will have pre-agreed the sort of questions to be asked and by which member of the panel.

At the first interview you may be asked questions that are similar to the ones that follow. After each question I have provided you with some tips on how to respond. You may also decide to take this workbook with you to the cases so that you can take notes on the following questions. These will act as a reminder of what you need to be looking out for.

SAMPLE QUESTION 1

What were your first impressions when you did your court observations?

This question is designed to assess firstly whether you have actually carried out any court observations and also what you learnt whilst you were there. My advice is that you attend at least two different court session sittings, more if you have the time. You should also try and see a variety of sittings and possibly in different courts. This will give you a far wider/ diverse understanding of how courts operate, the types of hearings you will be involved in as a magistrate and also the decisions that are made by the magistrates. I recommend that when you attend the court you first of all introduce yourself to the court clerk or usher. Inform them that you are applying to become a magistrate and you would like to sit quietly at the back and observe proceedings. You should take with you a small notebook and pen in order to take down anything that you learn on the day. Here's a list of things you may want to look out for during each visit:

- How the courtroom is set up

- What the proceedings involve for each case hearing

- How the defendant/accused is positioned within the court room

- The different people who are involved in the hearing

- The type(s) of cases you witnessed (try to get a variety)

- The questions asked by the magistrates to both the accused and also the other members of the courtroom during the decision making process

- Did anything surprise you about the proceedings?

- What punishment was passed and how you felt about the sentence/ fine

- What was your view of the decisions the magistrates made **and the reasons they gave?**

NOTES:

SAMPLE QUESTION 2

How would you have approached any of the decisions yourself if you were a magistrate?

I wanted to include this question as I believe it is highly likely it will be asked during your first interview. It is only natural to be surprised at some of the decisions magistrates make when sentencing or otherwise. What is important to understand is that magistrates are required to follow sentencing guidelines. You can find out more about these at the following website:

WWW.SENTENCINGCOUNCIL.ORG.UK

My advice, when responding to this question, is to have an understanding that decisions made by magistrates are based solely on the facts of the case and do not take into account bias, prejudice or personal feelings they may have. As a magistrate you should never pre-judge a person just because of how they look or how they act. You will be trusted to make decisions based on facts of the case and also be required to follow sentencing guidelines. If I was responding to this type of question I was say:

"I would have approached the decision making process in a logical, concise and professional manner taking into consideration the facts of the case. I would have also followed my training, listened to the views of the other magistrates I was sitting with, asked appropriate questions and also adhered to the sentencing guidelines. Any decisions that I took would be without bias, prejudice, pre-judgement or discrimination."

NOTES:

SAMPLE QUESTION 3

What impression did your form of the roles of all the other main 'players' in the courtroom?

During your court sessions you will have seen that, centrally, these are the defendant, court legal adviser, Crown prosecutor, defence solicitors, probation officers, police officers, prisoner escorts or possibly prison officers, witnesses and the press.

Having personally sat in during a number of court hearings I was surprised at a number of things. Firstly, I was surprised at the attitude of some of the alleged offenders. As a magistrate you will be required to keep control of the courtroom and sometimes this will mean a requirement to address inappropriate behaviour in court. Secondly, I was also surprised that the magistrates did not know a great deal about the law and were seeking advice from the court legal advisor. However, after attending these sessions I now understand that magistrates cannot be expected to know everything about the law, which is why you will see the presence of the court legal advisor in the courtroom. He or she is there to provide appropriate legal advice to the magistrates when required.

When you attend your court hearings I recommend you think about the above question and take notes on how you felt about the roles of each person/player in the room.

Key Tip

Take this workbook in to the court sittings that you attend and use it to take notes about the roles of each key player in the court room.

NOTES:

SAMPLE QUESTION 4

What do you think are the main crime problems in your area (or in the country)?

Having an understanding of crime problems in your area and the country as a whole is important. I can guarantee you will be asked a question that relates to this subject. There are a number of ways that you can find out about local crime issues and the most obvious one is through reading your local newspapers. I would also recommend visiting the website of your local police force as this will give up-to-date information relating to the problems in your area, and more importantly, what the police and community are doing to tackle these issues. I would also recommend carrying out an internet search for your local parish council. For example, if you reside in Kent, simply type in Google 'Kent parish council'. This will then bring up websites that relate to your local parish council areas. From these websites you will be able to glean information that relates to problems in the local area. You may even decide to attend one of the local parish council meetings in order to gain a better understanding of your area. Taking these extra steps will all work in your favour during the interview.

Key Tip

Show the panel that you have taken the extra effort to find out about the issues in your local area. Attending a local parish council meeting is an effective way of doing this.

In respect of learning about the key issues nationwide, I recommend that you:

- Read a good quality newspaper every day.
- Watch the evening news.
- Go to the website WWW.POLICE.UK; from here you will be able to search nationwide in order to find out about the local crime issues affecting each area.
- Visit WWW.STATISTICS.GOV.UK where you can find out up-to-date crime trends and statistics.

NOTES:

SAMPLE QUESTION 5

What factors do you think cause people to commit offences?

This is quite a difficult question to answer; however, I recommend that you approach it with a mature outlook. If you talk to some of your friends they may say that people commit crimes because they have a lack of respect for others, that they do not care and that they are a disgrace to society. My own personal view on the reasons and factors why people commit offences are as follows:

- It may be due to a lack of education and an understanding of what is expected of them in society. Some people do not understand the consequences of their actions. They may have experienced a difficult upbringing or may not have had a suitable role-model from whom they could learn.

- People also commit crimes due to sheer desperation when they feel they have no other avenue to choose. This may often be the case when they are using drugs or alcohol.

- People sometimes commit crime due to anger which has built up over long periods of time.

- People may commit crime when they feel they are not valued in society or amongst their peer groups. They may commit crime in an attempt to obtain *status* amongst others.

Obviously there are many other factors involved as to why people commit crimes. Use the box below to take some notes and detail what factors you believe cause people to commit crime.

NOTES:

SAMPLE QUESTION 6

What are your views on the recreational use of drugs?

This type of question can very easily catch you out. I must stress that it is very important you are honest when responding to the question. Here's how I would personally respond to this question:

"I personally believe that the recreational use of drugs has many negative effects. There is evidence to suggest that recreational drug use in on the rise. I believe that taking drugs can lead to physical or psychological dependence and as such all areas of a person's life can be affected by drug use. Relationships can break up due to arguments over drug use, or a person using drugs may be more likely to make mistakes at work. People are also more at risk of unsafe sex while under the influence of drugs and the risk of crime being committed rises considerably. There are, however, counter-arguments that state the use of recreational drugs should be legalised. My own opinion is that recreational drugs should never be legalised. I strongly believe that this would only lead to further crimes being committed and the effect it would have on society would be irreparable."

Key Tip

Demonstrate an understanding of how the use of recreational drugs can affect people and people within our society.

Now use the box below to write down your own views on the subject.

NOTES:

SAMPLE QUESTION 7

What particular factors do you think might give rise to youth crime?

There are a number of factors that can give rise to youth crime. Here are just a few:

- **Peer pressure.** This is where young people are sometimes pressurised by their friends and peers into carrying out acts they wouldn't normally do.

- **Lack of parental control.** Parents have a huge influence on the upbringing of their children. If the parent does not act as a suitable role model there is a chance the child will commit crime.

- **Boredom.** Unless the youth of our society are engaged in creative activities then there is a greater chance of crime being committed through boredom.

- **A lack of self-esteem.** Maslow's hierarchy of needs states that one of the basic human needs is that of status. Unless appropriately guided, some young members of our community will seek status through crime.

- **A lack of appropriate role models.** Unless young people have suitable role models to aspire to they may commit crime. For example, if a young person sees an older member of his or her peer group achieve status through drug dealing they may decide to choose this route as opposed to one of responsibility, hard work and education.

Key Tip

Read the local newspapers and pay particular attention to court cases and the reasons given for the offending. You will also be able to attending court sittings in order to gain an understanding to the factors that give rise to crime and youth crime in particular.

Now use the box below to write down your own views on the subject.

NOTES:

SAMPLE QUESTION 8

Have you (or somebody very close to you) ever been the victim of a crime and, if so, what was it and how did you feel about it?

This question is designed to see whether you understand how victims of crime feel and also your level of maturity and understanding of the situation. In order to provide you with suitable information to respond to this question, allow me to give you a fictitious scenario:

> *Your house has been burgled and a number of expensive and personal items have been stolen.*

If you read the above scenario, how does it make you feel? If you have previously been a victim of crime you will naturally feel a level of anger towards the person who has committed the crime. Let's assume that you have in fact been a victim of the above crime and you are a magistrate hearing a case which is very similar to the one you have personally experienced. How would it make you feel? No doubt you would sympathise with the victims, wouldn't you? The important thing to remember as a magistrate is you are required to act in a non-biased manner. You must make sound decisions based on the facts of the case and not allow your judgement to be clouded in any way or be influenced by your own experiences. Here's how I would personally respond to this question:

"Yes I have been a victim of crime and if I am honest it made me feel angry at the time. However, I fully understand that as a magistrate I must not allow my feelings to influence my judgement at any time. It is important that I make decisions in conjunction with the other magistrates based on my training and the guidelines provided."

Key Tip

Do not show any form of prejudice during the interview and try to demonstrate a level of maturity when responding to the questions.

Now use the box below to write down your own views on the subject.

NOTES:

- Shed & attempted break in.
- Saddened & even angry at the
time; even somewhat vulnerable °If I'm honest going forward.
as a woman living on my own.
- Built strong relationships
w/ my neighbours. Neighbour watch etc.
- Can't bring personal
experiences like that into the
court room.

→ Heartened by 2 facts

F Kelly → secondly,
neighbours   police.

- while it did upset me at
the time (what is written
opposite).

↙ not let   ↘ make
influence   decisions
judgment/   in conjunction
cloud mind.   w/ other
                          magistrates
                          based on
                          my training/
                          guidelines
                          provided.

SAMPLE QUESTION 9

Did your views change, and if so how, when you learned more about the defendants you saw appearing in court?

Remember here that people appearing before the magistrates are innocent unless and until proved guilty: so they only become 'offenders' if and when they are convicted and are about to be sentenced. If the situation arises, try to show that you understand this important difference.

Let me provide you with a fictitious scenario to test your level of prejudice (preconceived judgement):

There has been a serious accident involving two cars. The first car, a white Citroën Picasso, was being driven by a 50 year old male called Sebastian. Sebastian is a family man and a managing director of a local charity organisation. The second car, a black Vauxhall Nova GSi, was being driven by a 19 year old male called Wayne. Wayne is currently unemployed and has a previous conviction for driving under the influence of alcohol. Who do think has caused the accident?

Of course, the correct answer should be that you cannot decide who has caused the accident until all of the facts relating to the case are presented to you. However, to make my point, how does this scenario *really* make you feel? I can guarantee that many of us would pre-judge this situation and assume that Wayne had caused the accident. Under no circumstances should you ever act in a prejudice manner whilst working as a magistrate. You must base your decisions on the facts of each case that is presented to you.

Use the box below to take some notes on this question.

NOTES:

SAMPLE QUESTION 10

What is the best way to stop people: (a) offending in the first place and; (b) re-offending when sentenced?

I believe the most effective way to stop people from offending in the first place is through education, positive parenting and an understanding of what is expected of people in society.

I believe the most effective way to prevent re-offending when sentenced is through an intense period of education and rehabilitation. The following factors will also play a pivotal role:

ACCOMMODATION AND SUPPORT

A third of prisoners do not have settled accommodation prior to custody and it is estimated that stable accommodation can reduce the likelihood of re-offending by more than a fifth.

EDUCATION, TRAINING AND EMPLOYMENT

Having a job can reduce the risk of re-offending by between a third and a half.

IMPROVING HEALTH

Offenders are disproportionately more likely to suffer from mental and physical health problems than the general population and also have high rates of alcohol misuse.

THE USE OF DRUGS AND ALCOHOL

Around two thirds of prisoners use illegal drugs in the year before imprisonment and intoxication by alcohol is linked to 30% of sexual offences, 33% of burglaries, 50% of street crime and about half of all violent crimes.

FINANCE, BENEFITS AND DEBT.

Ensuring that ex-offenders have sufficient lawfully obtained money to live on is vital to their rehabilitation.

CHILDREN AND FAMILIES

Maintaining strong relationships with families and children can play a major role in helping prisoners to make and sustain changes that help them to avoid re-offending.

ATTITUDES, THINKING & BEHAVIOUR

Prisoners are more likely to have negative social attitudes and poor self-control. Successfully addressing their attitudes, thinking and behaviour during custody may reduce re-offending by up to 14%.

Now use the box below to write down your own notes in relation to this question.

NOTES:

SAMPLE QUESTION 11

What is your understanding of the basic and wider commitments of being a magistrate?

As a magistrate, you are required to sit for at least 26 half-day court sittings each year. A 'half-day' sitting typically lasts from 10am to 1pm or 2pm to 5pm, though you need to be there half-an-hour before to prepare. On some benches, sittings are organised on a full-day basis. You receive your schedule for sittings well in advance, but it is possible to rearrange sittings in an emergency. In addition, you will need to be available for training.

Key Tip

Have a thorough understanding of the role of a magistrate and be sure to have discussed the commitments required with your family and employer.

Now use the box below to write down your own notes in relation to this question.

NOTES:

SAMPLE QUESTION 12

How do you see yourself organising your life to meet those commitments?

This question is clearly designed to assess your level of commitment to the role. It is essential that you have thought about how you will organise your life to meet the commitment of becoming a magistrate.

Here's my own response to this question:

"I would make sure that I am fully prepared for the role by keeping an organised diary of my commitments. As far ahead as possible, I would keep my diary clear in order to meet my responsibilities. Although I have a relatively busy schedule at present I am extremely flexible and there is nothing in my working life that cannot be changed; therefore, I am 100% certain I can meet my commitments. In addition to maintaining an organised diary I have also discussed the role and the level of commitment required with my family. They are fully aware that I will working as a magistrate, if successful, and have pledged their support. Finally, I have considered carefully the level of commitment required and can assure you that I will have no issues meeting my responsibilities."

Now use the box below to write down your own notes in relation to this question.

NOTES:

SAMPLE QUESTION 13

Why do you want to be a magistrate?

I can guarantee that you'll be asked this question during the interview. Only you will know the exact reasons why you want to become a magistrate and it is important you are honest in your response. Here are my own reasons for wanting to become a magistrate:

"Over the last three years I have had the opportunity to carry out voluntary work within the community. This has been in the form of working at my local community centre for a few hours per week. I have learnt a tremendous amount during that time and it has opened my eyes to my local community.

I want to become a magistrate because I very much enjoy working in the community and the skills and experiences I have gained through my voluntary work would be very much suited to this role. I understand that the role of a magistrate is one that requires a high level of responsibility, coupled with the ability to make sound judgements and decisions. I have held numerous management positions during my career and I have very much enjoyed the responsibilities I have been entrusted with. I see the role of a magistrate to be very similar in that you are required to act with a high degree of integrity, trust and maturity and I have always excelled in these types of roles."

Now use the box below to write down your own response to this question.

NOTES:

SAMPLE QUESTION 14

If you want to volunteer a contribution to society, why do it in this particular role?

This question is once again assessing the reasons why you want to become a magistrate. Many people want to become magistrates for the perceived 'power' and 'status'. These are the people the Local Advisory Committee does not want to take on!

There are many other ways in which you can volunteer in society, so this question is a valid one. Here's my own personal response to this question:

"I believe I am at a point in my life where I have a tremendous amount of experience and the role of a magistrate is one that is taken very seriously. I have assessed and read the six key qualities and I feel that my own attributes are most suited to this role. Although I have a wealth of life experience to bring to the position I am also a committed learner and would enjoy the challenge of understanding the role of a magistrate. I have also some experience of working in other volunteer roles and I now feel that I am ready to take on more responsibility. The role of a magistrate is one that I feel I would enjoy and I would very much look forward to learning from the other experienced magistrates."

Now use the box below to write down your own response to this question.

NOTES:

SAMPLE QUESTION 15

What were the reactions of your family and employer when you said you were applying?

This question is designed to see how much support you are getting from your family and employer during your application. If your family or employer does not support you, you may not make it through to the second interview! The most effective way to obtain support is through communication. Talk to your family; talk to your employer and inform them both of the commitment required to carry out the role.

Key Tip

It is very important you have the support of your family and your employer during your application.

NOTES:

SAMPLE QUESTION 16

What would you get personally from being a magistrate?

Now here's a good question! To begin with, here's not what to say:

- The satisfaction of seeing people punished for their crimes.

- The status of being a magistrate amongst my peers.

- The power that the role can bring.

And here's what I would personally get from being a magistrate:

- the satisfaction of giving something back to society;

- an ability to make a difference to our community;

- a deeper understanding of our society and the problems we all face;

- working with a wide range of diverse people in the magistracy;

- personal development;

- the opportunity to develop my own skills;

- the opportunity to bring my own life experiences and skills to the bench.

Now use the box below to write down your own response to this question.

NOTES:

SAMPLE QUESTION 17

What would you bring to the role?

When preparing for this question I would write down a list of your own personal qualities. I would also write down the 6 key qualities that are required to become a magistrate and, if you possess those 6 key qualities, use them during your response. Here is a short list of positive things to say whilst responding to this question:

- Organised
- Committed
- Reliability
- Flexible
- Effective communicator
- Good listener
- Effective reasoning skills
- Effective listening skills
- Ability to see others point of view
- Quick leaner

Key Tip

Think about the qualities required to become a magistrate and use them during your response to this question, if you have them of course!

Now use the box below to write down your own response to this question.

NOTES:

SAMPLE QUESTION 18

What do you think the downsides might be of being a magistrate?

Personally, I cannot think of any downsides to becoming a magistrate!
Perhaps the lack of pay is a downside; however, this should not be a
problem for you as you will undoubtedly enjoy the opportunity to carry out
the role for no return, except for you expenses.

NOTES:

SAMPLE QUESTION 19

Do you think that the media is always right about crime?

The media are not always right about crime. Many newspapers may have a political agenda which can influence the manner in which they report. Whilst the media are to be respected, they do not always get it right in relation to crime, especially when it comes to sentencing! We have all read newspapers criticising the justice system for perceived lenient sentences. As a magistrate you will have no control over this; it will be your job to apply the rules and follow the relevant guidelines.

NOTES:

SAMPLE QUESTION 20

Do you yourself have any questions of the panel?

At the end of the interview you will be invited to ask questions of the panel. I would recommend asking one of two questions. Here's two that I would recommend asking:

Q1. Is there literature or information I can read about the magistracy whilst I am waiting to learn if I am successful or not? I am keen to find out more about the role if possible.

Q2. If I am successful I am very much looking forward to starting the training. Is there generally a long wait before the commencement of training?

NOTES:

SOME THINGS TO DO

- Make sure you are familiar with the ground to be covered at first interview;

- Think how you would answer questions such as those above;

- Think what other questions you would ask of a candidate at first interview if you were on the panel and then consider how you would answer them;

- Make a special effort to keep up-to-date with recent crime issues in your locality and nationally – you might well be asked for your views on some major issue which was in the media just a day or two before. Always try to give a balanced answer;

- Consider the issue of how the press report crime and court hearings;

- Think of what questions **you** might like answering – this may include something around the next steps in the appointments process and time scales if not already covered but do also try to think of something focused around the Six Key Qualities and how you would need to approach your duties – and don't sound too presumptive that you are past the first hurdle even if you get the feeling that you have done well!

THE SECOND INTERVIEW

If you have performed well enough at first interview (i.e. to at least the extent that the panel does not recommend against a second interview) you will be offered a second one, usually five to 15 working days later so the timescale may be tight.

The second interview will involve:

- discussing two previously unseen case study exercises that will be handed to you on arrival for the interview – around 30 minutes only will be allowed for you to think about how you will answer both - a ranking exercise and an individual case study (both as described further below) before going into the interview.

- an interview lasting about 40-50 minutes. The interview panel will again usually comprise three members (with at least one being a non-magistrate).

Membership may differ from the first panel, although there is sometimes one member from the first interview which will serve to ensure some carry over.

The above may sound a bit daunting but, again, remember that the panel is trying to see the 'real you' so, if you know what to expect, you should be able to give a good account of yourself.

THE FIRST CASE EXERCISE: RANKING THE SERIOUSNESS OF OFFENCES

The first exercise will give you around ten micro scenarios and you will be asked to rank them in order of seriousness as you see matters. There is no need to 'panic' as there is no 'right or wrong' answer, although:

- you will be asked to explain what you took into account in each scenario and why you ranked them in the way you did.

- you may be asked to comment on an opposing view of the ranking order.

- you need to show that you are prepared to listen to, and consider fairly, any contrary views the panel may put to you (don't feel devalued or overly defensive in your ranking as they may be taking a contrary view solely for the sake of the exercise. Whatever, be positive, but make clear that you understand differences of opinion, are open-minded and fully considering any counter-views, that you are not being 'precious' about your own view.

- you will need to reflect that there may be legal or guideline aggravating or mitigating factors (see e.g. the 2008 Magistrates' Court Sentencing Guidelines at WWW.SENTENCING-GUIDELINES.GOV.UK) that you must or must not take into account (you will later be trained in the use of these if you are appointed and need not learn them now).

- you should specifically consider the harm done or likely to be done by an offence and the level of the offender's culpability.

The scenarios might include, for example:

- assault on a police constable

- possession of drugs

- possession of indecent pictures of children

- domestic violence (by either partner)

- theft

- burglary.

More substantial examples appear in the 'Sample Ranking Exercise' provided within this section of your guide. In their way all will probably be serious and the basis of the exercise is to see what factors you think make up that seriousness and whether you can weigh say the effect of the theft of a purse from a pensioner by going into his or her house through an open door against the impact of domestic violence on a young child who might witness it going on between his or her parents. If you understand the nature and process of this exercise in advance you should have no difficulty in arriving at a measured response in readiness for discussion in the short time available. It is the way in which you arrive at your answer that will be important, not whether you have placed everything in some 'correct' order.

Expect to answer questions such as:

Q. Why do did you place [a particular choice] at the top of your list?

Q. What if the burglary was at night and the intruder had a weapon?

Q. Why did you place [a particular choice] after [another choice]?

SAMPLE RANKING EXERCISE

All interview panels set up by Advisory Committees will, at the second interview, use a form of Ranking Exercise approved by the Ministry of Justice. The actual format and content may vary but the basic task will be broadly the same:

1. From a list of ten or so briefly described offences you will be asked to pick say the four that you consider to be the most serious.

2. You will then be asked what factors in those four made you consider them to be the most serious – remember there will be no 'right or wrong' answer.

3. You may also be asked which you think was the most serious of the four you chose and why.

4. You may also be asked what factors you identified in the other six offences.

Important tips to consider

1. The facts will be straightforwardly and briefly stated for you – there should not be too much detail to get to grips with.

2. This exercise requires no prior knowledge of court work or sentencing – it is your own, immediate impressions that will be sought.

3. Although some offences may at the extremes be less serious than others it might help to identify and note briefly (using your own 'nudge' words) the salient features of each offence and then pick your four most serious:

   a) this way, and given the limited time available, you won't pick your four by gut reaction and then feel the need to spend precious time revising once you start listing the seriousness factors.

   b) magistrates are trained to analyse cases and facts before they reach any decision – this focuses the decision-making process and also helps with the reasons for the final decision.

4. Look for factors in the way offences were committed which make them more or less serious of their type and in relation to different types of offences.

5. Consider also any factors about the offender you may be given.

On the next few pages I have provided three sample Ranking Exercises for you to try. Write down your thoughts/observations in the 'relevant features' box and prioritise the 4 most serious (in your opinion) on the right hand side.

You will note that I have deliberately not provided the answers to the ranking exercise, simply because there are no correct answers! During the interview you will be required to explain why you have chosen your top 4.

SAMPLE RANKING EXERCISE 1

Facts	Relevant Features	Four Most Serious
Ambulance called to a young woman who has collapsed outside a nightclub. The girl's female companion is drunk, insults and shoves the crew, kicks in the headlight of their ambulance and is then arrested by passing police.		
A 35 year-old woman is stopped for drink-driving (just over the limit) on her way to collect her husband two miles away who missed the last bus home from work. It transpires that she is just about to finish a six-month driving ban for 'totting up', etc.		
A 40-year-old man has recently been released from prison having served three months for a sex offence on a child. Being a registered sex offender he told the police that he would be living with his mother on release. Instead he has gone to live with his girlfriend and her two young children		

Facts	Relevant Features	Four Most Serious
An 18 year-old sixth-former has been found to have 30 ecstasy tablets in his school bag. He claims that they were for personal use and he did not want his parents to find them at home.		
A 50 year-old man is passing an elderly widow's sheltered housing bungalow and sees the glass front door open and her handbag on the hall table. He sneaks in and steals the handbag which contains that week's pension money.		
Members at a local family tennis club smell cannabis and trace it to a 40 year-old coach who kept a small amount in his locker and smoked it between giving lessons to youngsters.		

Facts	Relevant Features	Four Most Serious
On a wet afternoon, a 55 year-old man, late for a business meeting, drives his new 4x4 at 42 mph in a 30 mph area near a school as the pupils are just leaving.		
A 30 year-old man has a row with his wife at home and pushes her against a cupboard causing her some bruising about the head and face.		
A 25 year-old woman who is a local heroin user walks out of her local supermarket with a DVD recorder under her arm and, when challenged by the security guard, knees him in the groin and tries to flee.		
A 30 year-old woman has a row with her husband in a pub and pushes him over a bar table causing him deep lacerations to his arm and back from broken glasses.		

SAMPLE RANKING EXERCISE 1
WITH RELEVANT FEATURES ADDED

Compare your notes to the following suggestions:

Facts	Relevant Features	Four Most Serious
Ambulance called to a young woman who has collapsed outside a nightclub. The girl's female companion is drunk, insults and shoves the crew, kicks in the headlight of their ambulance and is then arrested by passing police.	• Drunkenness is no excuse • Offence against public servant • Ambulance probably out of use for some time – possible effect on others who need emergency services • General public nuisance	?
A 35 year-old woman is stopped for drink-driving (just over the limit) on her way to collect her husband two miles away who missed the last bus home from work. It transpires that she is just about to finish a six-month driving ban for 'totting up', etc.	• Nature of offence even if just over the limit • Breach of earlier court order • Short distance (but many accidents occur near to home?)	?
A 40-year-old man has recently been released from prison having served three months for a sex offence on a child. Being a registered sex offender he told the police that he would be living with his mother on release. Instead he has gone to live with his girlfriend and her two young children.	• In breach of the sex offender register provisions either by not telling truth on release or changing mind and then not notifying	?

Facts	Relevant Features	Four Most Serious
An 18 year-old sixth-former has been found to have 30 ecstasy tablets in his school bag. He claims that they were for personal use and he did not want his parents to find them at home.	• Drugs in a school environment • Possible effect on younger pupils • Not charged as 'possession with intent to supply' but a lot of tablets for own use	?
A 50 year-old man is passing an elderly widow's sheltered housing bungalow and sees the glass front door open and her handbag on the hall table. He sneaks in and steals the handbag which contains that week's pension money.	• Opportunist and not forcible entry • Must have known victim likely to be elderly and possibly of limited means? • General effect of burglary on victims	?
Members at a local family tennis club smell cannabis and trace it to a 40 year-old coach who kept a small amount in his locker and smoked it between giving lessons to youngsters.	• Small amount and for personal use • Views on cannabis have varied • Effect on other members • Possibly children about	?

Facts	Relevant Features	Four Most Serious
On a wet afternoon, a 55 year-old man, late for a business meeting, drives his new 4x4 at 42 mph in a 30 mph area near a school as the pupils are just leaving.	• Not the highest of excess speeds • Brakes, steering etc. may be in excellent condition • But extra danger near school • Driver may have been concentrating on his lateness	?
A 30 year-old man has a row with his wife at home and pushes her against a cupboard causing her some bruising about the head and face.	• 'Domestic violence' in a private setting? • Male assaulting a female • A push or was it worse? • Injuries not the most serious?	?
A 25 year-old woman who is a local heroin user walks out of her local supermarket with a DVD recorder under her arm and, when challenged by the security guard, knees him in the groin and tries to flee.	• Nature of assault • Likely to have been children and families present	?
A 30 year-old woman has a row with her husband in a pub and pushes him over a bar table causing him deep lacerations to his arm and back from broken glasses.	• Female assaulting a male • 'Domestic violence' in a public setting • A push or was it worse? • Injuries quite serious	?

SAMPLE RANKING EXERCISE 2

Facts	Relevant Features	Four Most Serious
A 39 year old man is caught spraying graffiti on his ex-girlfriends car. He sprayed the words 'SLAG' over the bonnet of the car and smashed in the headlights. He has no previous convictions.		
A 26 year old woman is arrested for harassing her ex-boyfriend. She has been sending him between 60 and 70 abusive text messages every day for 2 weeks, despite his pleas for her to stop. She already has a caution relating to a previous boyfriend for harassment.		
A 40 year old Fire Officer is caught driving with no insurance. He has no previous convictions and claims that he thought his wife had renewed the insurance.		

Facts	Relevant Features	Four Most Serious
A 17 year old male youth is caught urinating over a war memorial statue in the town centre. When the police arrested him he said that he was drunk and that he did not know the statue was a war memorial. He is very upset and apologetic.		
A 33 year old man of no fixed abode was caught spraying racial and offensive graffiti across the window of a local Chinese restaurant. When questioned by police he informed them that the staff had given him a wrong take-away order. When he complained to them in a calm manner they refused to change it.		
A 19 year old male university student has been caught smashing the window of the local conservative office in his local town. When questioned by the police he said that he was angry at the increase in tuition fees.		

Facts	Relevant Features	Four Most Serious
A 42 year old tennis coach is arrested after a 15 year old girl, whom he has been coaching, complained about a number of lewd and suggestive text messages he had sent her. In the numerous text messages he had indicated that he wanted to meet up with her for sexual intercourse. He has no previous convictions.		
A 28 year old school teacher has been caught on school premises with cannabis in her handbag. She claims that it is for personal use only. She has no previous convictions.		
A 47 year old woman is arrested after hitting her unemployed husband over the head with a hammer after a row over unpaid bills. She has no previous convictions.		
A 19 year old man is arrested after punching a nightclub doorman in the face after he refused to allow him entry. The 19 year old man is on leave from the Army after serving 6 months in Afghanistan.		

SAMPLE RANKING EXERCISE 2
WITH RELEVANT FEATURES ADDED

Compare your notes to the following suggestions:

Facts	Relevant Features	Four Most Serious
A 39 year old man is caught spraying graffiti on his ex-girlfriends car. He sprayed the words 'SLAG' over the bonnet of the car and smashed in the headlights. He has no previous convictions.	• Are there any mitigating circumstances? • Severity of the offence. • Could lead to further incidents or attacks.	?
A 26 year old woman is arrested for harassing her ex-boyfriend. She has been sending him between 60 and 70 abusive text messages every day for 2 weeks, despite his pleas for her to stop. She already has a caution relating to a previous boyfriend for harassment.	• Previous conviction. • Number of messages excessive. • He has requested for her to stop.	?
A 40 year old Fire Officer is caught driving with no insurance. He has no previous convictions and claims that he thought his wife had renewed the insurance.	• Respected member of the community. • Should have known better? • Genuine mistake?	?

Facts	Relevant Features	Four Most Serious
A 17 year old male youth is caught urinating over a war memorial statue in the town centre. When the police arrested him he said that he was drunk and that he did not know the statue was a war memorial. He is very upset and apologetic.	• Mitigating circumstances? • Public unrest after an incident of this nature. • Alcohol involved. • Shows remorse.	?
A 33 year old man of no fixed abode was caught spraying racial and offensive graffiti across the window of a local Chinese restaurant. When questioned by police he informed them that the staff had given him a wrong take-away order. When he complained to them in a calm manner they refused to change it.	• Serious offence. • Mitigating circumstances?	?
A 19 year old male university student has been caught smashing the window of the local conservative office in his local town. When questioned by the police he said that he was angry at the increase in tuition fees.	• Serious offence of criminal damage. • No reason to take this sort of action.	?

Facts	Relevant Features	Four Most Serious
A 42 year old tennis coach is arrested after a 15 year old girl, whom he has been coaching, complained about a number of lewd and suggestive text messages he had sent her. In the numerous text messages he had indicated that he wanted to meet up with her for sexual intercourse. He has no previous convictions.	• Serious offence. • The intention is to carry out a sexual act. • He has suggested that they meet.	?
A 28 year old school teacher has been caught on school premises with cannabis in her handbag. She claims that it is for personal use only. She has no previous convictions.	• On school premise makes this more serious.	?
A 47 year old woman is arrested after hitting her unemployed husband over the head with a hammer after a row over unpaid bills. She has no previous convictions.	• Violent offence. • Mitigating circumstances of unpaid bills?	?
A 19 year old man is arrested after punching a nightclub doorman in the face after he refused to allow him entry. The 19 year old man is on leave from the Army after serving 6 months in Afghanistan.	• Alcohol involved. • Respected member of the community. • Serious offence.	?

SAMPLE RANKING EXERCISE 3

Facts	Relevant Features	Four Most Serious
A fire engine is attending a fire in a block of flats. A 17 year old male youth turns off the fire hydrant during firefighting operations for a joke to impress his mates.		
A 35 year old woman spits in the face of her neighbour after an argument over an overgrown garden hedge.		
An 18 year old girl was caught urinating in a shop front enclosure after a night out celebrating her University Degree results. When a police officer approached her she told the officer to "F#ck Off!"		
A 44 year old man is caught with indecent photographs of children on his PC. He has already served a 12 month sentence for a similar offence.		
A 55 year old man steals a bag of crisps from a local supermarket. He claims that he is unemployed and cannot afford to eat.		

Facts	Relevant Features	Four Most Serious
A 32 year old member of the Muslim Community throws a brick through the window of the local Conservative Office window. He has no previous convictions or offences.		
A 37 year old woman is late picking her two children up from school because she has been at lunch with her friends. On her way to school to pick up her children she is stopped for speeding at 35 mph in a 30 mph limit. The police breathalyse her and although she is not over the limit she has consumed alcohol.		
A 22 year old man is arrested after punching his girlfriend in the face after he catches her sending flirtatious texts to another man. He has a previous conviction for GBH.		

Facts	Relevant Features	Four Most Serious
A 61 year old woman is caught smoking in a public house. When challenged by the landlord she refuses to put out the cigarette. The police are called and she is arrested.		
A 30-year-old woman has a row with her husband in a pub and pushes him over a bar table, causing lacerations on his arm and back from broken glasses.		

SAMPLE RANKING EXERCISE 3
WITH RELEVANT FEATURES ADDED

Compare your notes to the following suggestions:

Facts	Relevant Features	Four Most Serious
A fire engine is attending a fire in a block of flats. A 17 year old male youth turns off the fire hydrant during firefighting operations for a joke to impress his mates.	• Severe incident? • Endangering life of the firefighters and residents. • Fire could spread due to lack of water causing considerable damage.	?
A 35 year old woman spits in the face of her neighbour after an argument over an overgrown garden hedge.	• Offence is serious. • Heat of the moment? • Whose hedge was it?	?
An 18 year old girl was caught urinating in a shop front enclosure after a night out celebrating her University Degree results. When a police officer approached her she told the officer to "F#ck Off!"	• Public disorder offence. • Swearing at a police officer more serious? • Alcohol involved.	?
A 44 year old man is caught with indecent photographs of children on his PC. He has already served a 12 month sentence for a similar offence.	• Serious due to repeat offender.	?
A 55 year old man steals a bag of crisps from a local supermarket. He claims that he is unemployed and cannot afford to eat.	• No excuse for theft. • Mitigating circumstances.	?

Facts	Relevant Features	Four Most Serious
A 32 year old member of the Muslim Community throws a brick through the window of the local Conservative Office window. He has no previous convictions or offences.	• Criminal damage to property. • No previous convictions.	?
A 37 year old woman is late picking her two children up from school because she has been at lunch with her friends. On her way to school to pick up her children she is stopped for speeding at 35 mph in a 30 mph limit. The police breathalyse her and although she is not over the limit she has consumed alcohol.	• She is under the limit, therefore she has not been caught drink driving. • Only just under the limit.	?
A 22 year old man is arrested after punching his girlfriend in the face after he catches her sending flirtatious texts to another man. He has a previous conviction for GBH.	• Serious repeat offence. • Mitigating circumstances?	?

Facts	Relevant Features	Four Most Serious
A 61 year old woman is caught smoking in a public house. When challenged by the landlord she refuses to put out the cigarette. The police are called and she is arrested.	• Relatively minor offence?	?
A 30-year-old woman has a row with her husband in a pub and pushes him over a bar table, causing lacerations on his arm and back from broken glasses.	• Was it intentional? • Injury makes this more serious.	?

THE SECOND CASE EXERCISE: A MORE DETAILED INDIVIDUAL CASE STUDY

The second exercise, which forms part of the second interview, will be a single, fuller case scenario, more than likely based on sentencing practice.

You will not be required to have any knowledge of sentencing aims, practices or actual disposals and there will, again, be no real 'right or wrong' answer.

It might, however, be worth being aware that there are the following four broad ascending levels of sentencing, each of which has its own sort of 'threshold' test:

- absolute or conditional **discharge** (i.e. re the latter, broadly no penalty unless there is reoffending)

- **fine** (based on both the seriousness of the offence and the offender's financial circumstances and up to £5,000 in more serious cases in the magistrates' court)

- **community order** (e.g. supervision by a probation officer, curfew order, undertaking a rehabilitative programme: this is now a generic order within which there can be various components of this kind)

- **imprisonment** (aka 'custody') (which can be suspended if appropriate).

Sometimes more than one sentence can be used at the same time but you will not be expected to know the ins-and-outs of this. The exercise will again test how you approach the problem.

What is important here are matters such as:

- how you deal with the overall decision-making process.

- what issues you identify as relevant.

- what you might be trying to achieve in sentencing.

- whether and how you think a pre-sentence report ('PSR') from the National Probation Service might assist in sentencing (what would you expect it to tell you that you have not already heard from the Crown prosecutor and the defence solicitor).

- where you would broadly pitch your sentencing.

- how you react to having to consider giving up to one third 'credit' or 'discount' against sentence for a (timely) guilty plea.

- whether you are able and willing to refer to guidance and to seek/take advice.

Again, you must be ready to explain your views and to listen attentively and respond to opposing views in a balanced way. Three example case studies appear at the end of this section.

The 'Good Character and Background' question will be put again, this time probably at the end of the interview.

You will again also be invited to ask questions.

It is at the end of the second interview that the panel will complete its formal assessment 'scores' and recommendations to the full Advisory Committee.

SOME THINGS TO DO

- Make sure you are familiar with the ground to be covered at the second interview;

- Think how you would answer questions on the above matters;

- Think what other questions you would ask of a candidate at second interview if you were on the panel and then consider how you would answer them;

- Make a special effort to keep up-to-date with recent crime issues in your locality and nationally – you might well be asked your views on some major issue such as the early release of prisoners, knife crime, or anti-social behaviour which was in the media just a day or two ago;

- Think how you might objectively approach a case of the kind you may have heard of or seen reported recently;

- Think of what questions you might like answering – again this may often include something around the next steps in the appointments process and time scales if not already covered but do also try to think of something more aimed at the Six Key Qualities and how you would need to approach your duties. Again, don't presume that you are through but be confident having prepared well in accordance with this guide.

SAMPLE CASE STUDY 1

Consider the following facts:

- Robbo is aged 18.

- He lives at home with his divorced mother who is supporting him financially during his full-time IT course at the local college.

- He has just pleaded guilty at the first hearing to three offences of racially aggravated criminal damage.

- Late one Sunday evening he had super-glued A3 size posters (which he had run off on the college's photocopier) on the windows of each of three shops in the local precinct, the Star of India Restaurant, Patel's Newsagents and Chinatown Takeaway

- The posters said 'Go back where you belong' and had pictures of the 'golliwogs' that used to feature on a certain brand of jam.

- It took a specialist cleaning firm most of Monday morning to remove the posters and clean the windows.

- He has no previous convictions.

- His course is due to finish in three months' time and he has just joined an agency to look for temporary office work for when he finishes.

How might you answer the following sample questions at interview (and what reasons would you give):

1.   At what level (say fine, community-based order or custody) would you normally pitch criminal damage by defacement which leaves no permanent damage (e.g. graffiti or fly-posting)?

2.   What makes the present offences more or less serious than other offences of criminal damage by defacement?

3.   Apart from the obvious inconvenience and cost, what sort of harm might have resulted from Robbo's offences?

4.   What personal factors about Robbo do you think might affect how you would want to sentence him?

5.   How would you feel if you were advised that you might be able base any financial penalty against Robbo on the fact that his mother is maintaining him at present?

6.   Allowing for the fact that you are not expected to have any technical knowledge about sentencing, what, in broad terms, would you like your sentence to look like?

7.   Assuming that Robbo's funds are limited, would you prefer to give priority to a fine, compensating the business owners or meeting the public costs of bringing the prosecution?

8.   How would you feel if advised that, because he has pleaded guilty at the first opportunity, you should reduce Robbo's sentence by around one third.

9.   How, if at all, would your approach differ if Robbo had previously been subject to an Ant-Social Behaviour Order (ASBO) for painting graffiti which expired 18 months ago?

In the half-hour you will have on the day to consider the above Case Study along with the Ranking Exercise you might find it appropriate again to make a few notes to 'nudge' you and on which to build in the interview. Try this with the sample exercise and try and stick to 30 minutes to 'get you in training'.

Compare what you noted down with how somebody else might have approached the case as described below:

1. **Usually a fine but community order (perhaps unpaid work) might be appropriate if e.g.**

   a) More serious in nature

   b) Previous convictions.

2. **Aggravated by e.g.**

   a) Racial element

   b) Number of offences

   c) Obviously pre-planned.

3. **Other harm would include:**

   a) Victims would feel racially offended

   b) Victims might fear personal attacks

   c) Effect on local community relations

   d) Other members of ethnic minorities might feel offended or in fear

   e) Possible loss of business.

4. **Personal factors might include:**

   a) Comparative youth

   b) Lack of means

   c) May 'grow out of it' once he has a job?

5. **Finances:**

    a) Obviously totally dependent on mother at moment and for immediate future

    b) Should not escape a financial penalty (if appropriate) just because he draws his means from someone else

    c) Equally mother should not be unduly penalised

    d) He may have a job in the near future

    e) Could look for some part-time work now.

6. **Broad sentence:**

    a) Community order perhaps with unpaid work and/or programme to address racial views

    b) Compensation to extent possible and permitted by guidelines

    c) Might look at custody if repeated.

7. **Priority:**

    a) Compensation

    b) Fine

    c) Costs.

8. **Reduction by a third:**

    a) Has saved time and the need for the victims to undergo the experience of giving evidence in court

    b) Would reduce if so required – reduction preferable to unpaid work but not a programme to address offending behaviour.

9. **ASBO:**

    a) Not in breach.

    b) But shows predisposition.

    c) May strengthen the need for more than a fine (what are the further facts?)

SAMPLE CASE STUDY 2

Consider the following facts:

- Peter is 47.

- He lives with his wife and two children and works as a checkout assistant at the local Tesco superstore.

- He has just pleaded guilty at the first hearing to one offence of theft. During a shift at work he was seen by the shop floor manager placing £40 in his pocket whilst the till was open. The act was caught on CCTV within the store.

- Over the last 12 months the store has seen an increase in money going missing from supermarket tills and, as a result. Installed covert CCTV cameras behind every till worker.

- Peter had a good work record until the incident. He has since been sacked from his job.

- He has no previous convictions.

- When interviewed by the police he stated that he was struggling to make ends meet at home and the bills were going unpaid. He had taken on a second job in the evenings as a bar worker to try and improve things but it wasn't enough.

How might you answer the following sample questions at the interview (and what reasons would you give)?

10. At what level (fine, community-based order, suspended sentence or custody) would you normally pitch theft?

11. Apart from the obvious financial loss to the store, what harm might have resulted from Peter's offence?

12. What personal factors about Peter and his situation do you think might affect how you would want to sentence him?

13. What are the mitigating factors in this case?

14. Allowing for the fact that you are not expected to have any technical knowledge about sentencing, what, in broad terms, would you like your sentence to look like?

15. How would you feel if advised that, because he pleaded guilty at the first opportunity, you should reduce Peter's sentence by around one-third?

In the half-hour you will have on the day to consider the Case Study along with the Ranking Exercise, you might find it appropriate to make a few notes to 'nudge' you and on which to build on during the interview.

Try this with the sample exercise and try and stick to 30 minutes to 'get you in training'.

Compare what you noted down with how somebody else might have approached the case as described below.

10. The sentencing guidelines for a theft of less that £17,500 indicate a sentence of up to 21 months. Due to the relatively small amount involved:

   a) Community order or suspended sentence.

11. Embarrassment to the store's reputation as the story is more than likely to be printed in the local newspapers.

12. He has a good working record to date. He is obviously a hard worker as he has taken on a second job in an attempt to make ends meet. He is unable to pay the bills at home.

13. Mitigating factors are:

   a) No previous convictions.

   b) Problems at home in respect of finances.

   c) Relatively small amount taken.

14. Sentence?

   a) Fine – although could he pay it?

   b) Community order.

   c) Suspended sentence.

15. Reduction by a third:

   a) Has saved time and the need for expensive trial in court.

   b) Would reduce if so required.

SAMPLE CASE STUDY 3

Consider the following facts:

- John is 21.

- He lives at home with his parents and works at a local charity shop. He is on minimum wage.

- He has just pleaded guilty at the first hearing to driving a motor vehicle when an accident occurred whereby damage was caused to another vehicle, failing to stop, failing to report the accident and driving without due care and attention.

- John has a good work record to date and his employer has stated that he will not lose his job. Character references have been provided by two people: John's former Head teacher and the Charity shop manager. Both state his actions were 'totally out of character'.

- He has no previous convictions.

- When interviewed by the police he stated that he became highly stressed after the incident and regretted deeply his actions.

How might you answer the following sample questions at the interview (and what reasons would you give)?

16. At what level (fine, community-based order, suspended sentence or custody) would you normally pitch this type of incident?

17. What harm might have resulted from John's offence?

18. What personal factors about John and his situation do you think might affect how you would want to sentence him?

19. What are the mitigating factors in this case?

20. Allowing for the fact that you are not expected to have any technical knowledge about sentencing, what, in broad terms, would you like your sentence to look like?

In the half-hour you will have on the day to consider the Case Study along with the Ranking Exercise, you might find it appropriate to make a few notes to 'nudge' you and on which to build on during the interview.

Try this with the sample exercise and try and stick to 30 minutes to 'get you in training'.

Compare what you noted down with how somebody else might have approached the case as described below.

16. A conviction of driving without due care and attention would usually bring 3 to 9 penalty points on the drivers licence. They will also face the possibility of a fine and Court Costs:

   a) Fined £75, ordered to pay a victim surcharge of £15 and costs of £43. His licence was endorsed with five points.

17. Embarrassment to this good reputation and the stress and worry for the victim whom he collided with during the accident.

18. He has a good working record to date and the character references provide evidence of his good reputation. He also deeply regrets the incident and the pleaded guilty at the earliest opportunity.

19. Mitigating factors are:

   a) No previous convictions.

   b) No person(s) injured as a result of the accident.

   c) John regrets his actions.

20. Sentence?

   a) Fine, victim costs and court costs.

FINAL TIPS AND ADVICE

- During both sets of interview it is very important that you are honest. The role of a magistrate is a highly responsible one, and as such, you must be truthful about your personal situation, the level of commitment you can provide and also your beliefs.

- As a magistrate you are required to be able to commit to a certain number of sittings and also be available for training. Think very carefully about these commitments and be 100% certain you can meet them.

- During the second interview there are no actual 'correct' answers to the ranking exercise and case study. However, you will be assessed on how you reached your conclusions and will be required to discuss the reasons for your decisions. You should be prepared to be challenged on your decisions. Remember that, as a magistrate, you are required to come to decisions jointly as a bench and you should have the ability to listen to others viewpoints.

- It is important that you present a positive and formal impression at the interview. I recommend that you wear a formal outfit for both interviews.

If you would like any further information and advice on how to become a magistrate please visit our website:

WWW.HOW2BECOME.COM

Good luck with your interview.

Kind regards
Richard McMunn

Printed in Great Britain
by Amazon